The Bernard and Irene Schwartz Series on American Competitiveness

Foreign Investment and National Security

Getting the Balance Right

Alan P. Larson
David M. Marchick

CSR NO. 18, JULY 2006
COUNCIL ON FOREIGN RELATIONS

Founded in 1921, the Council on Foreign Relations is an independent, national membership organization and a nonpartisan center for scholars dedicated to producing and disseminating ideas so that individual and corporate members, as well as policymakers, journalists, students, and interested citizens in the United States and other countries, can better understand the world and the foreign policy choices facing the United States and other governments. The Council does this by convening meetings; conducting a wide-ranging Studies program; publishing *Foreign Affairs*, the preeminent journal covering international affairs and U.S. foreign policy; maintaining a diverse membership; sponsoring Independent Task Forces and Special Reports; and providing up-to-date information about the world and U.S. foreign policy on the Council's website, www.cfr.org.

THE COUNCIL TAKES NO INSTITUTIONAL POSITION ON POLICY ISSUES AND HAS NO AFFILIATION WITH THE U.S. GOVERNMENT. ALL STATEMENTS OF FACT AND EXPRESSIONS OF OPINION CONTAINED IN ITS PUBLICATIONS ARE THE SOLE RESPONSIBILITY OF THE AUTHOR OR AUTHORS.

Council Special Reports (CSRs) are concise policy briefs, produced to provide a rapid response to a developing crisis or contribute to the public's understanding of current policy dilemmas. CSRs are written by individual authors—who may be Council fellows or acknowledged experts from outside the institution—in consultation with an advisory committee, and typically take sixty days or less from inception to publication. The committee serves as a sounding board and provides feedback on a draft report. It usually meets twice—once before a draft is written and once again when there is a draft for review; however, advisory committee members, unlike Task Force members, are not asked to sign off on the report or to otherwise endorse it. Once published, CSRs are posted on the Council's website.

Council Special Reports in the Bernard and Irene Schwartz Series on American Competitiveness explore challenges to the long-term health of the U.S. economy. In a globalizing world, the prosperity of American firms and workers is ever more directly affected by critical government policy choices in areas such as spending, taxation, trade, immigration, and intellectual property rights. The reports in the Bernard and Irene Schwartz series analyze the major issues affecting American economic competitiveness and help policymakers identify the concrete steps they can take to promote it.

For further information about the Council or this Special Report, please write to the Council on Foreign Relations, 58 East 68th Street, New York, NY 10021, or call the Communications office at 212-434-9400. Visit our website at www.cfr.org.

CONTENTS

FOREWORD

The Dubai Ports World controversy has shed light on the tensions between Congress and the executive branch over the appropriate balance between foreign investment and national security. In the past few months, members of Congress have met with international companies, homeland security experts, and administration officials to better understand the process of security reviews of foreign investment in the United States. Congress is intent on changing the process and becoming more involved in it; the challenge ahead is to reform the process in order to minimize the security risks raised by foreign investment without discouraging future investment.

In this Council Special Report, Alan P. Larson and David M. Marchick discuss the benefits of foreign direct investment in the United States and the security risks posed by foreign ownership of certain U.S. assets. They examine the inner workings of the committee that conducts security reviews—the Committee on Foreign Investment in the United States (CFIUS)—and recommend what policymakers should and should not consider in reforming it. The authors acknowledge that a lack of transparency in the process mixed with a new security environment, in which foreign ownership is seen as more politically sensitive, has cast doubt over the nature and effectiveness of the process, and they offer suggestions on how best to address congressional concerns. At the same time, they argue that CFIUS has been more effective than is commonly assumed and warn against alleged cures that promise to be far worse than any "disease" that currently exists.

This Council Special Report by Alan Larson and David Marchick is part of the Bernard and Irene Schwartz Series on American Competitiveness and was produced by the Council's Maurice R. Greenberg Center for Geoeconomic Studies. The Council and the center are grateful to the Bernard and Irene Schwartz Foundation for its support of this important project.

Richard N. Haass
President
Council on Foreign Relations
July 2006

v

ACKNOWLEDGMENTS

The authors are grateful to the members of the Council Special Report advisory committee, which met twice over the course of the project to offer their comments on the outline and draft of the report—Guillermo S. Christensen, Elliot J. Feldman, Joseph H. Flom, Kristin J. Forbes, Peter M. Garber, Carl J. Green, Jessica R. Herrera-Flanigan, Rebecca K. Hersman, Robert D. Hormats, Merit E. Janow, Arnold Kanter, Brett B. Lambert, Marc Levinson, David A. Lipton, Daniel B. Prieto, Alfred J. Puchala Jr, Celina B. Realuyo, and Jeffrey R. Shafer. Last, but certainly not least, we thank Guy F. Erb for chairing the committee and offering constructive criticism on several versions of the report.

The authors thank Douglas Holtz-Eakin, director of the Maurice R. Greenberg Center for Geoeconomic Studies, for his oversight of the process from beginning to end. We also thank Council President Richard N. Haass for producing this Council Special Report and Director of Studies James M. Lindsay for his input. The authors also thank Patricia Dorff and Molly Graham in the Publications department, Lisa Shields and Brittany Mariotti on the Communications team, and Chad Waryas of the Maurice R. Greenberg Center for Geoeconomic Studies for their efforts in the production and dissemination of this report.

The authors would also like to thank the Bernard and Irene Schwartz Foundation for their generous support of this report.

Alan P. Larson
David M. Marchick

COUNCIL SPECIAL REPORT

INTRODUCTION

Despite the significant benefits that foreign investment brings to the U.S. economy, a recent poll by the Pew Research Center for the People and the Press found that 53 percent of Americans believe foreign ownership of U.S. companies is "bad for America," a sentiment that reached a boiling point with the proposed acquisition of the U.S. port operations of P&O Steam Navigation Company by Dubai Ports World (DPW). The DPW case brought to the public's attention the little-known executive committee charged with reviewing the security risks of foreign investment—the Committee on Foreign Investment in the United States (CFIUS)—and ignited a flurry of congressional activity to change its mandate and operations under the Exon-Florio Amendment to the Defense Production Act of 1950.

The United States has strong interests in both protecting national security and fostering the economic benefits associated with an open investment climate. In practice, these interests clash in only a few circumstances. Yet it is in precisely these circumstances that CFIUS must get it right. On the one hand, it is critical that CFIUS identify and mitigate national security risks associated with particular investments. On the other hand, when investments are blocked, politicized, or unnecessarily delayed, the United States sends a negative signal to the rest of the world about the openness (or lack thereof) of its markets. For every transaction that is consummated, dozens of others are considered, debated, and analyzed in boardrooms around the world. If the United States sends the wrong signals, CEOs and boards of directors of foreign companies may simply decide that the risks are too great to invest in certain sectors in the United States, costing the United States jobs and economic growth. Thus, the critical issue for policymakers debating CFIUS reform is as follows: How do you design an investment review mechanism that is rigorous enough to identify—and, if necessary, block—those transactions that truly threaten U.S. national security interests while not impeding those investments that do not? This Council Special Report addresses this important policy issue.

A Brief History of Foreign Investment and U.S. National Security

The link between national security and foreign investment has long been debated in the United States. During and after World War I, Congress passed legislation that restricted foreign ownership in specific sectors such as broadcasting, civil aviation, and shipping. These restrictions were established in reaction to perceived national security threats at the time. In some cases, such as in the telecommunications sector, restrictions on foreign ownership and control have gradually been eased. In sectors such as transportation, shipping, and broadcasting, the original investment restrictions remain in place.

In the 1970s, alarm over petrodollar investments from oil-producing nations led to congressional hearings and the creation of CFIUS, a twelve-agency committee chaired by the Department of the Treasury, which would be charged with reviewing acquisitions that could potentially threaten U.S. national security interests (see Appendix A).

In the late 1980s, serious public concerns arose about the growing level of Japanese investment in the United States, concerns driven by high-profile acquisitions of American-owned and -controlled firms and cultural icons like the Rockefeller Center. In cases like the semiconductor sector, the transfer of ownership and control from American corporations (e.g., Fairchild) to Japanese firms (e.g., Fujitsu) was widely viewed as a threat to American competitiveness. Existing export-control laws and regulations governing dual-use technologies were criticized as being inadequate in the context of foreign-owned firms. However, as Congress deliberated on these issues, the focus of the debate gradually shifted from concerns about economic competitiveness toward those acquisitions where foreign ownership might threaten national security.

This series of events was the background against which Congress enacted the Exon-Florio Amendment to the Defense Production Act of 1950 as part of the Omnibus Trade Act of 1988. Exon-Florio empowered the president to block mergers and acquisitions of U.S. companies by foreign firms when such takeovers threatened national security and where that threat could not be addressed effectively through other laws and regulations.

CFIUS has recently received a great deal of attention in reaction to two proposed acquisitions of U.S. assets by foreign companies: that of Unocal by the China National Offshore Oil Corporation (CNOOC) and that of the port operations of P&O Steam Navigation Company by DPW. While the president normally can count on significant deference from Congress on national security issues, in these two cases Congress either preempted a transaction before it was considered by the executive branch (in the case of CNOOC) or effectively overturned the executive branch's approval of a transaction (in the case of DPW) by forcing the foreign investor to abandon its acquisition of assets in the United States. The DPW transaction, in particular, has created the impression abroad that the traditionally ironclad U.S. policy of openness toward foreign investment may be softening.

However, even before the DPW controversy, CFIUS's work was criticized in several reports by the Government Accountability Office (GAO), an independent congressional agency. To their credit, members of Congress, particularly Senator Richard Shelby (R-AL), the chairman of the Senate Banking Committee, also began to focus on the issue well before CFIUS gained notoriety in policy circles as a result of the DPW transaction. According to GAO, CFIUS's shortcomings included a bias against proceeding to an extended review, known as an "investigation," and its too narrow definition of "national security." Other alleged problems with Exon-Florio included the lack of an understanding of and support for the CFIUS process in Congress; the lack of an agreed-upon process for congressional oversight; the ambiguous role of the White House in a process grounded in national security; the additional strains imposed by the new security challenges following the attacks of September 11, 2001; and the fact that National Security Agreements (NSAs) imposed on foreign companies by CFIUS as a condition for approving a transaction have placed foreign companies at a competitive disadvantage. Each of these problems is discussed in greater detail below.

The sense of uncertainty about the U.S. commitment to an open investment regime has been heightened by several initiatives, now pending in Congress, to amend the Exon-Florio Amendment. Legislation under active consideration in Congress would, if enacted, profoundly change the way CFIUS examines proposed U.S. acquisitions by foreign companies. If done right, the process can be improved either through legislation or an executive order; however, a number of bills currently being debated in Congress, including the bill recently passed by the Senate, could potentially discourage foreign investment without improving national security.

An important fact overlooked in the debate over CFIUS reform is that only a small fraction of foreign direct investments in the United States actually require CFIUS review. In the last few years, CFIUS has reviewed between forty and sixty-five transactions out of the more than 1,000 foreign acquisitions of U.S. enterprises made annually. Despite the fact that these sixty or ninety transactions represent a tiny fraction of overall foreign direct investment in the United States, congressional actions to block the DPW transaction and alter Exon-Florio have created the impression abroad that the United States is retrenching from its traditional open-investment policy.

IMPORTANCE OF BALANCING ECONOMIC AND SECURITY INTERESTS

There are two fundamental reasons why it is important that Congress and the administration effectively balance the twin objectives of maintaining openness to foreign investment and protecting national security. First, both the economic health of the United States and its long-term security depend on maintaining a welcoming environment for the majority of foreign investments. Second, if the United States creates a restrictive foreign investment climate marked by unnecessarily cumbersome regulatory reviews, other countries will surely follow that course, with real costs to the United States.

Foreign investment in the United States plays an important role in maintaining the vitality and vibrancy of the U.S. economy.[1] In 2003, U.S. affiliates of foreign investors employed 5.3 million workers in the United States, or about 5 percent of the U.S. workforce. On average, and particularly within major manufacturing subsectors with significant numbers of foreign-controlled firms, U.S. affiliates of foreign firms pay higher annual wages and salaries than their domestically owned competitors. Further, foreign investors spend heavily on research and development (R&D) in the United States, which creates high-skill, high-wage jobs that might not have been created otherwise.

In addition, the United States depends heavily on continued inflows of foreign investment because U.S. saving is insufficient to finance domestic investment. In 2005, the U.S. current account deficit was slightly more than $800 billion and growing, implying that the United States needed to import more than $2 billion each day to close the gap between domestic investment and savings.

But most foreign investments do not raise real national security concerns. It is hard to see how a Canadian acquisition of a real estate or retail chain, or a Dutch acquisition of Ben and Jerry's ice cream raises national security threats. By contrast, foreign investments in the defense sector or in certain parts of the information technology sector may raise real concerns. Because of the clear economic benefits from foreign investment, Congress needs to ensure that any amendments to Exon-Florio enhance CFIUS's ability to pinpoint those few transactions that raise genuine national security issues while not discouraging other foreign acquisitions that enhance the competitiveness of the U.S. economy without affecting national security.

IMPLICATIONS ABROAD

Debates are taking place in many countries between advocates of openness to foreign investment and proponents of restrictiveness. In several European countries, for example,

---

[1] Edward M. Graham and David M. Marchick. *U.S. National Security and Foreign Direct Investment* (Washington, DC: Institute for International Economics, 2006).

politicians have blocked several proposed takeovers and advocated the creation of national champions in specific sectors. Politicians in France have reacted with alarm to the New York Stock Exchange's proposed takeover of Euronext. As these debates continue, the course the United States takes will influence the development of new laws and policies abroad. Russian officials, for example, recently stated that they are watching developments in the United States closely. China plans to introduce its own CFIUS-like process later this summer. Countries could use the U.S. example to restrict capital flows under the pretext of enhancing security.

NATIONAL SECURITY REVIEWS OF FOREIGN INVESTMENTS

Exon-Florio is a unique piece of legislation. It gives the president sweeping authority to block a proposed private sector acquisition on his decision alone; no action by Congress is necessary. No court can review the president's decision, and there is no statute of limitations, meaning the president could unwind a transaction that was never reviewed by CFIUS years after it closes.

Under the law, the president must base his decisions on national security concerns even though the term "national security" is not defined. Instead, the statute enumerates several factors for the president to consider in making a national security determination, but leaves it to the president to define what national security is. This approach is consistent with American law and practice, which generally grants great authority on national security issues to the president.

SECURITY RISKS OF FOREIGN INVESTMENT

Why would foreign ownership and control of a U.S. company, in itself, raise security concerns? After all, foreign firms operating in the United States are subject to U.S. laws, including export control, espionage, and labor laws. Moreover, many global companies—the same companies that are the largest investors—are owned by large pension or institutional funds, reducing or eliminating the "national" character of such companies.

Rightly or wrongly, there is a perception in some parts of the U.S. government that American-owned and -controlled companies are more likely to abide by the spirit of U.S. government laws, regulations, and policies. In some cases, concern about a foreign acquisition may be linked to evidence that the foreign company is subject to the control or influence of a foreign government, one whose aims may be hostile to the United States. In still other instances, concerns may be related to the need for the company to work with U.S. security or intelligence agencies and to handle sensitive information prudently.

In some narrowly defined instances, the nationality of a firm making an acquisition may raise security issues that need to be examined and, where necessary, addressed. For example, in the defense sector, the Department of Defense (DOD) has long utilized myriad tools to ensure that American citizens handle classified work performed by contractors. In the telecommunications sector, the Department of Justice (DOJ) requires that American citizens handle wiretapping requests and other demands for data for law-enforcement purposes.

In most sectors of the U.S. economy, however, the nationality of the equity owners of a global corporation makes no difference whatsoever from a national security perspective. It is hard to see why foreign ownership of real estate, retail, or agriculture businesses, for example, could threaten U.S. national security interests. The challenge for CFIUS, therefore, is to determine which acquisitions raise real security issues and, if possible, to determine how to mitigate those security concerns.

THE CFIUS REVIEW PROCESS IN PRACTICE

The Exon-Florio legislation imposes strict time lines for reviews of foreign investments. These time lines, including a thirty-day initial review and, where necessary, a subsequent sixty-day, second-stage "investigation" and presidential decision-making period, create predictability in the process. The initial thirty-day period parallels the same thirty-day period for an initial antitrust review under the Hart-Scott-Rodino Act, thereby allowing both foreign and domestic companies making acquisitions to secure approval within the same time period. Under the statute, investors will receive a yes or no decision from CFIUS within no more than ninety days.

In practice, flexibility has been built into the system. When the committee cannot resolve concerns within these time lines, CFIUS agencies have pressured companies to withdraw their applications, noting that with more time an application might be approved, and cautioning foreign investors that if CFIUS is forced to abide by the statutory time frames, the decision would likely be negative. Additionally, in most cases, parties to a transaction engage in extensive prefiling consultations with CFIUS. The DPW controversy created the false impression that the reviews completed during the initial thirty-day period are cursory; in fact, in most cases, CFIUS can conduct a rigorous national security analysis of a transaction prior to and during the initial thirty-day review period.

Another example of the statute's flexibility is that filings by companies are not mandatory. CFIUS has encouraged foreign companies proposing to acquire U.S. assets to seek approval whenever they have reason to believe that the acquisition might raise national security issues. The Department of the Treasury, which chairs CFIUS, and other federal agencies have frequently met with acquirers to discuss whether a filing is appropriate, although post-DPW CFIUS has, in an abundance of caution, stopped providing guidance to parties on the propriety of a filing.

The principle of voluntary filings was established because Congress and past administrations wanted to avoid the specter of investment "screening," a process in which there is a mandatory review of all foreign investments. The United States historically has objected to the screening policies of other countries and has fought hard to moderate or eliminate the effects of such policies through the U.S.-Canada and U.S.-Australia Free Trade Agreements, among others.

Despite the voluntary nature of CFIUS filings, the Exon-Florio Amendment gives investors a compelling incentive to notify CFIUS of any acquisition that might affect U.S. national security: unless the transaction parties engage in misrepresentation during the review process, once an acquisition is approved by CFIUS, it benefits from a regulatory "safe harbor," immunizing it against subsequent reviews or action by the president. However, if an acquisition is not submitted to CFIUS and that acquisition subsequently raises national security concerns, Exon-Florio gives the president the authority to force divestiture at any time, even long after the transaction has closed. To avoid that situation, investment banks and lawyers routinely advise acquirers to file with CFIUS if there is any possibility that a transaction might raise national security issues.

CFIUS has numerous options for mitigating national security concerns raised by individual deals short of a formal recommendation to the president to block such a transaction. For example, the negotiation of a National Security Agreement between the acquirer and one or more of the CFIUS security agencies can help both sides to isolate and resolve those aspects of a transaction that might otherwise adversely affect national security. Agreements of this kind have become increasingly common in recent years.

The negotiation of a NSA follows a standard pattern. First, the agencies holding relevant national security responsibilities identify their concerns with particular aspects of the transaction. If necessary, the agencies let it be known that these concerns could lead them to oppose the acquisition and recommend to the president that the transaction be blocked. Such statements can set the stage for a discussion of measures, short of blocking the acquisition, to resolve the security concerns at issue. The security commitments offered by the acquiring party in the course of these discussions are then enshrined in a NSA. Frequently, these security commitments, including penalties for noncompliance, encompass obligations well beyond the requirements that domestic companies face under generally applicable laws or regulations.

Further, CFIUS agencies develop and implement compliance programs to ensure that companies live up to their obligations under NSAs. For example, in the defense industrial security sector, CFIUS and the DOD have, over the years, developed protocols and policies for addressing the potential national security impact of foreign ownership and control of companies with access to classified contracts, such as the establishment of a separate, secure subsidiary to handle classified contracts. These restrictions can impose significant economic costs and reduce efficiencies for the merged companies, but the requirements have become a well-established and accepted cost of doing classified work for the Pentagon. While CFIUS can be a hurdle and the security requirements often are formidable, defense firms have understood and accepted the process and the rules of engagement.

CFIUS TIME LINE/PROCESS

Informal consultations/briefing

	CFIUS reviews intelligence data, conducts analysis, asks questions	
Thirty-day review initiated at any point by filing notice with CFIUS	Internal CFIUS discussions to identify any national security issues	**Thirty-day review initiated at any point by filing notice with CFIUS**
	If national security issues exist, can they be mitigated?	

If yes, negotiate NSA, if necessary		If no, inform parties	
Agreement reached during thirty-day initial review	No agreement during initial thirty-day review	Continue process	Withdraw CFIUS notice if filed; abandon transaction

Forty-five-day CFIUS investigation

Agreement reached	No agreement

CFIUS approval

Report to president
Presidential decision fifteen days after report
Report to Congress

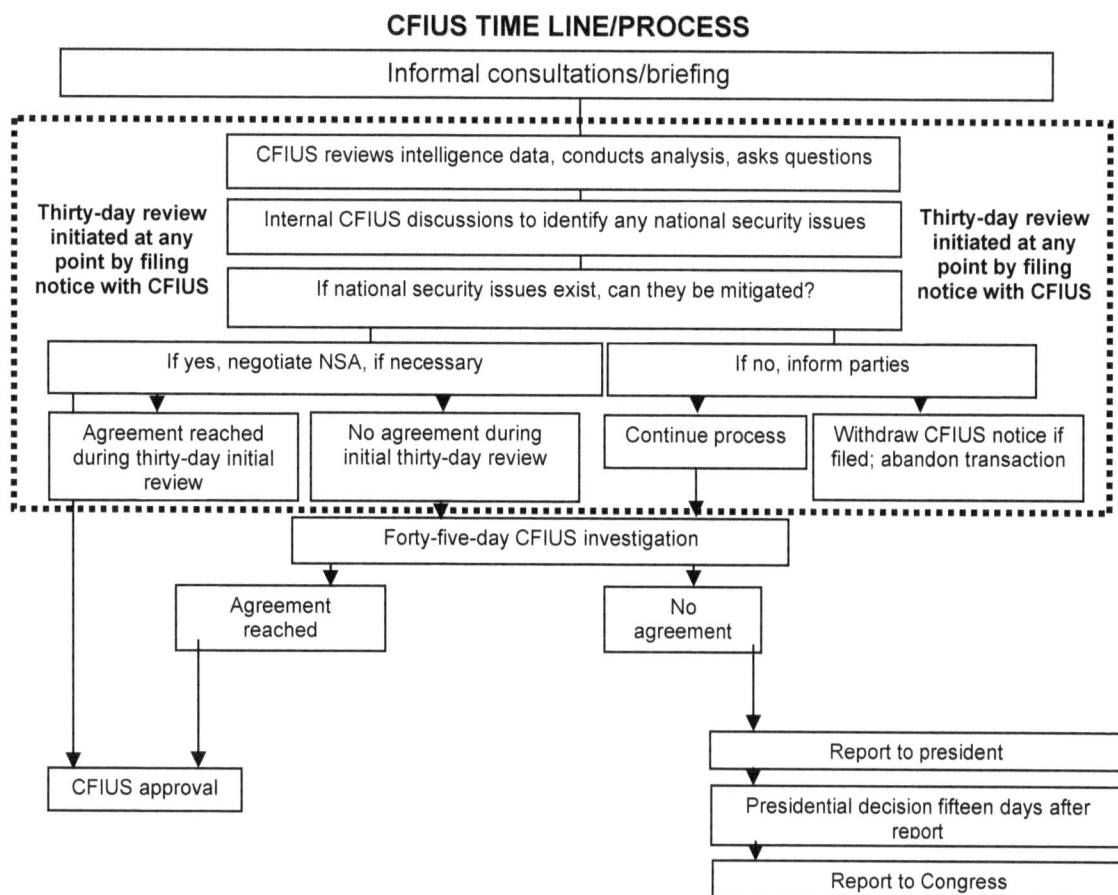

CRITICISMS OF THE CFIUS PROCESS

One of the main criticisms of CFIUS is that it has been a rubber stamp for foreign acquisitions. More specifically, critics of CFIUS have argued that because it is chaired by the Department of the Treasury, the committee does not give national security concerns the weight they deserve. That criticism fails to take into account either the enhanced security role of Treasury in recent years or the fact that CFIUS procedures require the chair to accommodate the interests of all agencies, including those with security expertise and responsibilities.

While it is true that the Department of the Treasury's primary mission is economic, the argument that it forces CFIUS to give security concerns short shrift is not well founded. Treasury has been a full member of the National Security Council (NSC) process for several years, has its own intelligence capabilities, and participates in the interagency intelligence community discussions. Furthermore, in recent years, new challenges—such as cutting the flow of financing to terrorist organizations and bolstering the economies of U.S. allies in the war on terrorism—have increased its security focus.

More importantly, the Department of the Treasury regularly defers to the agency with the greatest interests and expertise on particular transactions—the DOD for defense acquisitions; the DOJ for telecommunications acquisitions; and the Department of Homeland Security (DHS) for other acquisitions of critical infrastructure assets—to shape both the national security analysis and to negotiate and enforce the security agreements that are often utilized to mitigate specific national security concerns. In addition, CFIUS's structure and procedures empower individual agencies, including those departments whose primary mission is security or law enforcement. Under CFIUS procedures, one agency alone can insist on an investigation—the second-stage review conducted by CFIUS—into the national security implications of any given transaction. Moreover, while CFIUS occasionally produces split recommendations, arguments of comity and a desire not to put the president in the difficult position of choosing between security concerns and the economic priorities of an important foreign ally have created strong pressures for unanimity. In practice, however, the agency that raises the greatest concerns or that insists on moving to the investigation stage will virtually always get its way. In other words, in a consensus process, the agency position that forms the lowest common denominator usually prevails. This leverage, which can be exerted by one agency, is even more apparent in a post-DPW environment, where any stigma previously associated with going to a second-stage investigation has evaporated.

As evidence of CFIUS's alleged inattention to national security, critics often cite the fact that in only one case—that of a Chinese acquisition of a U.S. aerospace company in 1990—has the president exercised the authority under Exon-Florio to formally block an acquisition. This isolated example, however, does not do justice to CFIUS's record of deterring or mitigating transactions that raise, or even potentially raise, national security issues. For example, on many occasions, would-be acquirers have withdrawn CFIUS applications after being informed by Treasury or another CFIUS agency that there would be a unanimous recommendation to the president to block the acquisition. While the data collected by Treasury are limited, since 1997 at least thirteen transactions have been withdrawn and not refiled by foreign companies. By voluntarily withdrawing its application, a company can avoid the damage its business reputation would suffer from a formal decision by the president to block its transaction because of insurmountable national security concerns. In other cases, after informal consultations with CFIUS made clear the difficult path to regulatory approval, transactions have been abandoned before a CFIUS filing was ever made.

In sum, Exon-Florio has been a powerful, flexible, and effective tool for protecting national security, albeit one that occasionally imposes significant costs on foreign investors. Despite some initial hiccups soon after the legislation was adopted, sophisticated foreign investors from Europe and Japan, including those investing in sensitive sectors such as defense, learned how to anticipate and address U.S. security needs. Foreign acquisitions—even in sensitive sectors—continued to grow, and security issues were addressed, usually quite effectively, in the process.

PROBLEMS IN THE SYSTEM

While we disagree with many of the criticisms mentioned above, even before the DPW controversy, the foreign investment review process had a number of problems. CFIUS's failure to respond to congressional inquiries about the nature of the review process fostered an atmosphere of distrust and uncertainty in Congress concerning the adequacy of the process. CFIUS resisted efforts to brief Congress on particular transactions to preserve the confidentiality of the process. As CFIUS learned in the DPW transaction, agencies resist congressional requests for information at their peril. Furthermore, the White House's hands-off approach toward security reviews—which became obvious during the DPW controversy—contributed to Congress's perception that the CFIUS process failed to seriously consider real security concerns raised by specific transactions. Finally, CFIUS has often imposed burdensome requirements on foreign companies that similarly situated domestic firms can avoid, creating an uneven playing field for foreign investors in the United States.

The Lack of Transparency in the CFIUS Process

CFIUS operates outside the limelight and—for strong policy and confidentiality reasons—has, in the past, resisted requests by members of Congress to brief them on the details of controversial transactions. Thus, when the controversy over DPW's proposed acquisition arose, members of Congress were primed to criticize a process that lacked strong congressional support and awareness.

This problem arose in part because, while Congress clearly delegated to the president the authority to review individual transactions, Congress and the executive branch never reached an understanding on an appropriate role for Congress in the CFIUS process, particularly with respect to congressional access to information. This lack of clarity exists despite the fact that, under Exon-Florio, Congress created an exception for itself from the confidential treatment of filings made to CFIUS and details on the decisions of the CFIUS agencies. In other words, while CFIUS agencies are prohibited under law from disclosing information provided by parties about a transaction, this non-disclosure requirement does not apply to Congress. However, while the statute was clear that CFIUS was not required to withhold information from Congress, it did not articulate clearly what information CFIUS was required to provide to Congress with the exception of a quadrennial report and notice anytime the president personally made a decision on a transaction.

Most legislators today agree that Congress should not be involved in specific transactions. However, a growing number of congressional members want to have greater visibility into how the review process works, if not into the decisions made by CFIUS on specific transactions. As discussed below, clarifying the role of congressional oversight is at the heart of the current legislative initiatives.

The Role of the White House in the CFIUS Process

In addition to the tensions in the executive branch's relationship with Congress, the White House's role in the CFIUS process has also remained ambiguous. For example, although six White House offices are members of CFIUS (see Appendix A), the White House generally has chosen to take a hands-off approach, as it tends to do in regulatory matters, until issues come to the president for decision.

The White House's traditionally hands-off approach to the CFIUS process has been, of course, very different from the role it plays in many other national security issues. Typically, the National Security Council, operating under the direction of the president, sets the agenda and organizes interagency discussion of national security matters. NSC staff and other White House advisers participate fully and freely in the deliberative process.

The White House's arm's length approach to CFIUS has had the positive effect of contributing to an apolitical review process, one that has usually enabled complex issues to be assessed technically. At the same time, its approach has created a situation in which the president appears to be out of the loop on what are increasingly regarded as important national security questions. This issue came to the fore in the DPW case, when the administration publicly acknowledged that the president, vice president, secretary of treasury, secretary of homeland security, and secretary of defense were not briefed on the regulatory review process. It is not surprising that such decisions are made at the subcabinet level since subcabinet-level officials handle consequential issues daily. However, in the DPW case, the lack of White House ownership of the issue, combined with the lack of support or understanding of CFIUS within Congress, enabled opponents of the DPW transaction to question not only the merits of CFIUS's decision to approve the acquisition, but more importantly, to cast doubt on the integrity of the CFIUS process itself.

Uneven Playing Field for Foreign Investors

As already noted, security agreements negotiated in connection with CFIUS approvals often impose obligations on foreign companies that similarly situated domestic companies are not required to adopt, even if the same security concerns apply. In practice, Exon-Florio gives the security agencies (DOD, DOJ, DHS) leverage through which they can impose security conditions on foreign companies that they cannot impose on U.S.-owned companies. In many cases, these conditions represent sound security practices and advance legitimate and important policy objectives. However, because they apply only to foreign companies, they create an uneven playing field, albeit one that acquiring companies usually will accept as the price of admission into the American economy. At the same time, foreign companies that believe they have received rough treatment by CFIUS are increasingly asking their home governments to impose similar conditions on American companies. This backlash recently occurred in India after the Indian telecommunications company VSNL complained to the Indian government about the CFIUS process, and the Indian government in turn proposed security restrictions on foreign telecommunications companies operating in India. Thus, this asymmetrical treatment of foreign companies will likely create policy problems abroad for the same agencies that comprise CFIUS.

NEW SECURITY AND ECONOMIC CHALLENGES

During the past five years, a combination of new factors has added to stresses and tensions created in the original 1988 legislation. The new security challenges posed by 9/11 have raised concerns about foreign investments in areas deemed as critical infrastructure and have also heightened public scrutiny of investments from parts of the world that have not made major investments in the United States. Furthermore, the reliance of the United States on capital inflows and the growing capital surpluses of China and countries in the Persian Gulf—not previously major investors in the United States—have combined to create a volatile mix of politics surrounding some CFIUS cases.

Post-9/11 Security Environment

The CFIUS process has been put under strain by the new security environment created by 9/11. These attacks changed many things, including perceptions of the relationship between foreign investment and national security. Whereas CFIUS has long had clear and established protocols for dealing with foreign acquisitions of companies in the defense industrial base, in the post-9/11 environment, the committee has had to develop and implement new policies to protect critical infrastructure. This concurrent pursuit of policy development and implementation led to inevitable friction, particularly with respect to acquisitions of companies in the sectors deemed by DHS as "critical infrastructure."

Even before 9/11, telecommunications investments typically engendered CFIUS scrutiny, especially after the Telecommunications Act of 1996 eased restrictions on foreign ownership. The report of the 9/11 Commission made clear the importance of electronic surveillance and intelligence collection to protect the United States against future terrorist attacks. Consequently, agencies with intelligence or law enforcement responsibilities—which were already concerned about the possible implications of foreign ownership and control of telecommunications facilities—started to look even harder at proposed acquisitions in the telecommunications sector. Officials wanted, among other things, stronger assurances that foreign acquirers of telecommunications or electronics firms would cooperate fully with U.S. authorities' surveillance activities and that foreign ownership of telecommunications assets would not become a conduit for surveillance on behalf of foreign powers.

The attacks of 9/11 also prompted a rethinking of how the transportation system—on land, at sea, and in the air—could be used to threaten national security. Under the Patriot Act and other post-9/11 legislation, new law enforcement requirements were placed on firms in sensitive sectors, foreign as well as domestic, operating on U.S. territory. The attacks also affected public attitudes in ways that were not always aligned with government analyses or policy. For example, in the DPW case, the administration concluded—correctly, in our view—that the transfer of terminal ownership from one foreign-owned company to another did not raise security concerns. In fact, the administration correctly argued that the investment by DPW would have enhanced security by ensuring that DPW cooperated with U.S. security initiatives not only in the United States but at its port in Dubai. Nevertheless, many in Congress and the public were easily persuaded that terminal facilities operated by a state-owned company from the United Arab Emirates posed a security risk.

CHANGING PUBLIC PERCEPTIONS TOWARD FOREIGN INVESTMENT

Unease about foreign acquisitions today undoubtedly stems in part from the fact that some companies now considering acquisitions in the United States come from China, the Middle East, and other countries. In some cases, the public may perceive these countries as unsympathetic to U.S. interests. The companies themselves are not well known to Americans and do not know the American market well. Many of these companies do not have brand names that are firmly established in the United States. Some of these firms may need to go through a learning process similar to that which enabled Japanese companies such as Honda to become woven into the fabric of American communities.

But just because these companies are fairly new to the U.S. market does not mean that investments from such countries should be regarded as threats to national security.

More significant than the nationality of potential new investors is the fact that many of the companies from China and the Middle East are government owned and, in some cases, government controlled. The majority of publicly traded Chinese companies, for example, continue to be government-owned and -controlled. Many Chinese companies, though nominally private, remain under government influence, if not government control. In certain cases, government ownership and control can create national security issues, particularly when the foreign company's decisions become an extension of the government's policy decisions rather than the company's commercial interests. For example, the Russian energy giant Gazprom's decision to cut off gas supplies to the Ukraine in early 2006 was correctly characterized (and criticized) as driven by the Kremlin's desire to demonstrate its dissatisfaction with policies emanating from Kiev.

At the same time, government ownership of global corporations is not uncommon in Europe and Asia. And, in some cases, government ownership may be described as passive. Thus, it is important to separate ownership from control, and equally important to determine, on a case-by-case basis, whether government ownership of U.S. assets will create real national security issues. These issues are precisely what CFIUS was designed to tackle, and CFIUS already has the authority to subject acquisitions by certain government-owned and -controlled corporations to special scrutiny, particularly when the investments are flowing from countries not particularly sympathetic to U.S. interests.

ENERGY SECURITY

Over the past few years, energy policy has once again come to be seen in terms of national security. Rising oil prices, growing competition for supplies from China and India, and political uncertainties in major oil-producing countries such as Russia, Venezuela, Iraq, and Iran have revived the energy security concerns of the 1970s. Given the tightness of global energy markets and the instability and uncertainty in many significant energy-producing countries, the U.S. government does have significant national security interests in preserving the integrity of global energy markets. Similarly, the U.S. government has obvious national security and nonproliferation interests at stake in the nuclear energy sector. Thus, CFIUS's scrutiny of foreign investments in certain energy subsectors is appropriate. At the same time, foreign ownership of U.S. energy assets is only a small piece of the energy security equation. Equally important are cooperative, global efforts to diversify sources of energy, expand efficient energy use, and facilitate cooperation in responding to oil supply disruptions. Unfortunately, because of the lack of decisive action and a comprehensive national strategy on energy security, energy security concerns have become commingled with ones about foreign ownership of energy companies.

THE IMPORTANCE OF MAINTAINING AN OPEN INVESTMENT REGIME

Despite these concerns, the United States has a strong interest in attracting more foreign direct investment for economic and security reasons. Furthermore, the path chosen by the United States could influence the decisions of foreign governments currently considering reforms to their own internal review processes.

Security Benefits of Foreign Investment

Foreign investment can be part of the answer to the new security challenges. For example, foreign investments can contribute to infrastructure modernization and development of technologies in the United States. Alternatively, a foreign acquisition may make it possible for a defense supplier to remain in the United States or may lead to enhanced investments in a particular division of a major defense company that has not been a strategic priority for that company.

Economic Benefits of Foreign Investment

The United States has a strong interest in attracting more foreign direct investment. Foreign investors tend, on average, to pay higher wages, to invest significantly in local research and development, and to bring managerial innovations that contribute to American competitiveness.[2] Interestingly, the Japanese investments of the 1980s—which were an important motivating factor behind the enactment of Exon-Florio—today are viewed largely with equanimity by U.S. politicians and the public generally. Japanese affiliates in the automotive sector now account for almost 50 percent of U.S. production of cars and close to 20 percent of U.S. trucks. Without investments from Asia and Europe, employment and production levels in America's automotive industry clearly would be much lower than they are today.

Further, in a period of large U.S. current account deficits, maintaining a healthy balance between foreign investments in physical, as opposed to liquid, assets is also in the U.S. interest. There is always a risk that large foreign holdings of liquid U.S. assets could, if disposed of rapidly, destabilize the dollar and U.S. interest rates. However, when foreign firms, including firms from China and the Persian Gulf, make physical investments in the United States, they create a more permanent stake in the health of the U.S. economy.

The Stakes for American Investments Abroad

The U.S. approach toward foreign investment can easily affect U.S. companies' investments abroad. This too should be a matter of interest for all Americans, not just corporations or investors. Foreign investments in U.S. companies make a profound contribution to American exports, jobs, and economic vitality.

Foreign investments by U.S. companies drive American exports. Close to one-third of American exports flow to the affiliates of the same companies. American manufacturing firms invest abroad to market their products and services, as well as to

---

[2] Graham and Marchick, *U.S. National Security and Foreign Direct Investment.*

conduct R&D. Access to foreign markets through foreign direct investment creates jobs in the United States.

What is true in the case of manufactured products is even more so when it comes to services. Foreign investments and acquisitions by U.S. companies are an indispensable factor in exporting services. And, as the share of services in the U.S. economy increases, America's exports of services—banking, insurance, legal, and many others—have outstripped manufacturing exports in terms of their growth rate.

Finally, foreign investments, including acquisitions, are critical for the nation's access to raw materials, including oil. For years, the majority of America's oil needs have been met from foreign sources. Given the uniquely sophisticated technology that U.S. energy companies possess, overseas investments and acquisitions by those companies are a vital factor in determining whether oil supplies rise at a rate sufficient to meet growing demand.

An unnecessarily restrictive approach to foreign investment in the United States may simply encourage other countries to take actions of their own limiting the opportunities for American investors. Some countries may argue, falling back on the Third World rhetoric of the 1970s, that their security depends on maintaining control of the "commanding heights" of the economy, such as the banking or telecommunications sector. Other countries may argue that their oil reserves are a national security asset that should be owned and controlled only by the government or by nationals of that country.

Other countries will watch closely how Congress and the administration address the question of amending Exon-Florio. France, which has for some time practiced investment screening, recently tightened its rules. Russia and China are doing the same. Closer to home, Canada and Mexico, which are significant export and investment markets for American companies, have also debated new restrictions. From these examples, it is easy to see how changes in the Exon-Florio statutory and regulatory scheme have the potential to adversely affect how American companies are treated abroad.

TOWARD CFIUS REFORM

In the wake of the DPW transaction, more than twenty bills were introduced in Congress to reform the CFIUS process, prohibit foreign government ownership in port operations, or prohibit foreign ownership in broad swaths of the U.S. economy. Two bills—one in the House of Representatives, authored by Representatives Roy Blunt (R-MO), Deborah Pryce (R-OH), Carolyn Maloney (D-NY), and Joe Crowley (D-NY), and one in the Senate, authored by Senators Richard Shelby (R-AL) and Paul Sarbanes (D-MD)— recently approved in the House and Senate will form the basis for new legislation if the House and Senate can reconcile the differences in their approaches.[3]

Both bills seek to enhance CFIUS's accountability by requiring senior administration officials to sign off on decisions personally, clarifying CFIUS's authority to negotiate and enforce security conditions imposed on particular transactions, changing the time lines for reviews, and improving communication with Congress. On the last two issues, however, the bills take divergent approaches. The Senate bill gives CFIUS the option of adding an additional thirty days to the process *before* CFIUS decides whether to pursue an investigation. This proposed change creates the possibility that garden-variety CFIUS reviews could last sixty days instead of thirty. By contrast, the House bill gives CFIUS the option of adding time *after* an investigation, thereby ensuring that CFIUS has the flexibility to focus on the difficult cases while quickly clearing the easy ones. In addition, the Senate bill requires CFIUS to provide detailed reports to Congress and governors on *pending* cases, risking politicization of the process. By contrast, the House bill takes a more sensible approach modeled on other legislation, including Hart-Scott-Rodino antitrust reviews, by requiring CFIUS to issue detailed, semiannual reports to Congress. As discussed below, on both issues, the House bill will better enable CFIUS to protect national security while not impeding foreign investment that does not raise real security concerns.

---

[3] On July 26, 2006, the House approved the National Security Foreign Investment Reform and Strengthened Transparency Act of 2006 (H.R. 5337) by a vote of 424-0. On the same day, the Senate passed the Foreign Investment and National Security Act of 2006 (S. 3549) by voice vote.

More broadly, Congress should keep the following developments in mind as it debates changes to Exon-Florio.

CFIUS has already made a number of important adjustments and procedural changes in the wake of the DPW controversy. CFIUS agencies have made it clear to companies and their advisers that they expect advance prefiling briefings and consultations to ensure CFIUS has adequate time for reviews. Improvements have also been made in intelligence analysis, which is now being coordinated by the director of national intelligence, who consults with each of the relevant U.S. intelligence agencies. Transactions are also getting much higher-level attention in each of the CFIUS agencies. The departments of Homeland Security and Justice have implemented a more comprehensive process for tracking and monitoring security agreements. Finally, CFIUS has provided Congress with more frequent and detailed briefings, including briefings on a case-by-case basis after CFIUS completes a review. Thus, even without legislation, reform of the process is already under way.

Notwithstanding these improvements, Congress could further reform the process by passing the right type of legislation. Congressional action could help create greater confidence in the CFIUS process by putting a new congressional imprimatur on it. This imprimatur will be particularly important to help avoid another DPW-like blowup in Congress. At the same time, particularly after an issue explodes, as happened with the DPW transaction, Congress frequently overreacts, causing damage to U.S. economic and security interests. The goals of congressional action should be to:

1. Improve transparency and clarify the oversight role of Congress.
   - If Congress had more visibility into the process, there would be greater comfort and understanding that the national security review process is already rigorous. CFIUS agencies should spend more time on the Hill briefing members of the relevant committees on their activities, processes, and trends in filings.
   - CFIUS agencies should issue regular reports to Congress; these reports should give Congress real insight into how the CFIUS process works, the types of

security agreements CFIUS utilizes, and the types of transactions CFIUS is scrutinizing.

- However, CFIUS should keep sacrosanct proprietary business information, and should be judicious with respect to the provision of transaction-specific information to Congress.

2. Retain the existing timetables for review and investigation.

- Proposals to extend the existing time frames for CFIUS reviews, for example, by giving CFIUS the option of extending its initial thirty-day review period by another thirty days, should be rejected. The existing time limits work well because they balance the need for the agencies to have sufficient time to conduct reviews with the concomitant need for parties to an acquisition to have the certainty that they will receive a decision from CFIUS within a reasonable period of time. In addition, most companies that file with CFIUS—thereby starting the statutory clock—do so only after engaging in extensive informal consultations with the committee. Through these informal consultations, CFIUS agencies have additional time to assess the national security risks and design mitigation strategies, if necessary. Indeed, it is common for security agreements to be hammered out before the parties file a formal notice with CFIUS.

- In the majority of transactions reviewed by CFIUS, there are either no national security risks or a particular national security threat can readily be mitigated. These transactions can appropriately be approved by CFIUS in the initial thirty-day review period provided by statute. Moreover, if CFIUS needs additional time, it can and should proceed to the second-phase investigation. As was noted previously, following the DPW controversy, any stigma associated with moving to a second-phase investigation has evaporated. Indeed, in the first six months of 2006, CFIUS has already launched twice as many investigations as it did in all of 2005.

- Similarly, there seems to be consensus in Congress that acquisitions by government-owned companies should automatically be required to proceed to an investigation. Acquisitions by some government-owned companies unquestionably raise unique national security issues and should receive heightened scrutiny. But not all acquisitions by government-owned companies create the same national security risk. CFIUS should have the discretion to distinguish between transactions that raise issues and those that do not. Additional time does not necessarily equate with additional scrutiny; CFIUS should have the discretion to focus intensively on those transactions that raise real national security issues while expeditiously processing transactions that do not.

As Congress moves forward, there are also a number of potential pitfalls that it should avoid:

1. Do not incorporate "economic security" criteria.

   - Economic security, or variations thereof, has been proposed close to a half-dozen times since 1988, including when Exon-Florio became law. Indeed, the original bill offered by Senator James Exon (D-NE) would have authorized the president to block transactions that threaten the "essential commerce" of the United States. It would be difficult for CFIUS to implement a statutory requirement to protect "economic security," since the term is extraordinarily vague. Indeed, there is good reason to believe that an "economic security" test would simply become a vehicle for domestic industries seeking to block foreign competition.

2. Do not allow Congress to force an investigation or to override presidential approval of a particular transaction.

   - Such proposals raise serious separation of powers issues under the U.S. Constitution. In addition, these approaches would create so much uncertainty about the prospect of congressional involvement in the review process that a substantial number of foreign investors would simply not invest in the United States. Congress has a legitimate and important oversight role in ensuring that the Exon-Florio statute is implemented correctly. But Congress should not itself become a regulatory agency. By comparison, Congress has not overridden and should not override antitrust decisions made by DOJ or the Federal Trade Commission (FTC). It should not assume such authority in the CFIUS process.

3. Do not create a public notice requirement for Exon-Florio reviews or require broad and mandatory notification to governors.

- CFIUS reviews should remain confidential. Notification of pending transactions only invites further politicization of the process and creates risks that the process could be used for competitive, as opposed to national security, reasons.

4. Do not create a presumption that foreign investments in critical infrastructure create a national security risk.

- The Senate bill requires that foreign investments in critical infrastructure must proceed to a second-phase investigation unless a mitigation agreement has been put in place. By requiring a mitigation agreement to avoid a second-phase review, the bill creates the presumption that all foreign investments in critical infrastructure raise national security issues. While the debate over how to define critical infrastructure continues, the operative definition, contained in a March 2003 DHS report, covers twelve broad sectors that together constitute 25 percent of the U.S. economy.[4] The administration and Congress should work together to determine how best to protect critical infrastructure, regardless of who owns a particular company. Security policies and guidance could be developed on a sector-by-sector basis. A baseline level of security requirements should be established. And if there are particular national security issues associated with foreign ownership in a particular asset, CFIUS is well equipped to mitigate that risk or to block the investment. But until policies and doctrines with respect to critical infrastructure have been further developed, it is both dangerous and unnecessary to do anything beyond adding "critical infrastructure" as a factor that CFIUS should consider.

5. Do not remove the Department of the Treasury from the chairmanship of CFIUS.

---

[4] These sectors are: agriculture and food, water, public health, emergency services, defense, telecommunications, energy, transportation, banking and finance, chemicals, postal services and shipping, and information technology.

- The Treasury-chaired CFIUS process provides a full opportunity for security concerns to be raised, vetted, and addressed. A change of chairmanship (i.e., to the NSC) would result in a period of disruption and disorganization that would be as likely to weaken as to strengthen national security. Finally, changes in the chairmanship of CFIUS will inevitably be interpreted as signaling a dramatic change toward a more restrictive policy on foreign investment.

Congress has taken a deliberate approach toward CFIUS reform by holding hearings, circulating draft bills, and holding public markups of legislation. Still, Congress always risks overreaching when legislating in a heated political environment. Regardless of whether Congress acts this year to amend Exon-Florio, the president should issue an executive order to improve implementation of the current Exon-Florio statute. Such an executive order should:

1. Clarify the working procedures of CFIUS to enhance accountability;
2. Enhance transparency of the CFIUS process;
3. Require that Treasury provide Congress with an annual report on CFIUS's activities;
4. Provide monitoring of compliance with NSAs; and
5. Direct the National Security Council and the National Economic Council to support Treasury's efforts to ensure that national security and intelligence issues are effectively addressed.

ACTIONS FOR INTERNATIONAL LEADERSHIP

In addition to resisting legislation that chills legitimate foreign investment, the Bush administration should actively communicate continuing U.S. openness to foreign investment, including the fact that the majority of foreign acquisitions do not require a review by CFIUS. For example, the White House should issue a statement on foreign investment policy, along the lines of previous statements by the Carter and Reagan administrations, making clear that the United States welcomes foreign investment.

The recent controversies over particular proposed acquisitions of U.S. companies were undoubtedly fueled by fear of the unknown. More specifically, foreign investment in critical infrastructure from China and the Persian Gulf is a relatively new phenomenon; it is understandable that such investments raise questions or concerns in the minds of ordinary Americans that simply do not arise when firms from traditional allies like Britain or Canada acquire U.S. assets. Rather than being primarily a security threat, investment from newly industrializing countries should be seen as an important opportunity. Companies from such countries that seek to become global players will need to quickly learn the skills of adapting to foreign regulation and integrating into the communities in which they invest. By encouraging and helping them to do so, the United States and its allies can contribute to market-oriented development in these important emerging economies.

Further, one of the most important issues in the DPW case was the fact that DPW was owned and controlled by the firm's host government. The United States should continue to press for privatization of state-owned companies on both economic and national security grounds. CFIUS, however, is not the proper venue for this effort. For both economic and political reasons, the United States cannot afford to discourage relations or investments from companies in Europe, Asia, or the Middle East that still retain substantial government ownership. But as noted above, it is likely that government-owned foreign firms will inevitably draw heightened scrutiny from CFIUS in the future.

The administration and Congress also need to recognize and explain to the American public that, in many instances, greater homeland security depends on greater cooperation with foreign firms, not less cooperation. The United States cannot, for example, secure its skies without the cooperation of other countries' international passenger airlines and foreign airport authorities. Port security depends on international efforts like the Container Security Initiative, and energy security depends on multilateral cooperation to ensure that international energy markets function based on market forces and not according to the particular needs of an individual government. With that in mind, the United States should take the lead in bringing newly important energy consuming countries like China and India into the network of cooperative energy security arrangements such as the International Energy Agency. The United States and others must persuade China that its energy security lies not in seeing that its companies lock down arrangements with suppliers, but in developing a flexible domestic energy economy supported by a range of energy suppliers. As an incentive for cooperation with the United States, the administration should make it clear that if a foreign company is working effectively with U.S. authorities on international security arrangements, that will be a positive factor taken into consideration with any acquisition that company may be contemplating in the United States.

Finally, the United States should also promote discussion in the Organization for Economic Cooperation and Development (OECD) to identify international best practices in addressing security concerns effectively and in a manner consistent with open investment policies. However, pursuit of an internationally binding agreement would *not* be productive. In the 1990s, an ambitious U.S.-led effort to negotiate a legally binding OECD investment agreement, the Multilateral Agreement on Investment (MAI), foundered, largely in the face of French resistance. A similar effort today would probably be no more successful. Nevertheless, there is room for a more modest effort to articulate common, tried, and tested principles that could guide national legislatures and executive branch officials. Such an effort would draw on the OECD's ongoing work, through the Center for Cooperation with Nonmembers, with such countries as China, India, and Russia. This project would be an especially appropriate one to launch at the beginning of the tenure of the OECD's new secretary-general, Mexico's Angel Gurria. Gurria's experience as Mexico's finance minister has given him firsthand experience of the importance of foreign direct investment as a stable source of capital for a dynamic developing economy.

CONCLUSION

A small fraction of foreign direct investments in the United States raises genuine concerns regarding national security, thus requiring CFIUS review. As noted earlier, in the past few years, CFIUS has reviewed only forty to sixty-five transactions per year. Nevertheless, congressional pressure to block the DPW transaction and alter Exon-Florio has created the impression abroad that the United States is radically retrenching on its traditionally open investment policy.

Our recent travels in Europe, Asia, and the Middle East have shown us the level of concern felt by foreign investors about the current political environment in the United States. Other countries are closely watching the next steps of Congress and the administration. European investors are concerned that the traditional pattern of large investments in both directions across the Atlantic may be broken by protectionist pressures in Washington; Chinese investors fear that Chinese investment in the United States is not welcomed; and cash-rich investors in the Persian Gulf express concerns about the reaction they might provoke by proposing an investment or acquisition in the United States. While some adjustments in Exon-Florio may be necessary to restore the confidence of Congress, legislators should use a scalpel, not a chain saw. CFIUS has proved to be—and continues to be—an effective tool for vetting the national security concerns associated with foreign investment. If Congress fails to achieve the right balance, U.S. companies and workers could feel the repercussions for years to come.

APPENDIX

APPENDIX A

Agencies Represented on the
Committee on Foreign Investment in the United States

Executive Departments

- Department of Treasury (Chair)

- Department of Commerce

- Department of State

- Department of Homeland Security

- Department of Justice

- Department of Defense

Executive Office of the President

- Office of Management and Budget

- Office of the U.S. Trade Representative

- Council of Economic Advisers

- Office of Science and Technology Policy

- National Security Council

- National Economic Council

APPENDIX B

MISSION STATEMENT OF

THE MAURICE R. GREENBERG CENTER FOR GEOECONOMIC STUDIES

Founded in 2000, the Maurice R. Greenberg Center for Geoeconomic Studies at the Council on Foreign Relations works to promote a better understanding among policymakers, academic specialists, and the interested public of how economic and political forces interact to influence world affairs. Globalization is fast erasing the boundaries that have traditionally separated economics from foreign policy and national security issues. The growing integration of national economies is increasingly constraining the policy options that government leaders can consider, while government decisions are shaping the pace and course of global economic interactions. It is essential that policymakers and the public have access to rigorous analysis from an independent, nonpartisan source so that they can better comprehend our interconnected world and the foreign policy choices facing the United States and other governments.

The center pursues its aims through:

- Research carried out by Council fellows and adjunct fellows of outstanding merit and expertise in economics and foreign policy, disseminated through books, articles, and other mass media;

- Meetings in New York, Washington, DC, and other select American cities where the world's most important economic policymakers and scholars address critical issues in a discussion or debate format, all involving direct interaction with Council members;

- Sponsorship of roundtables and Independent Task Forces whose aims are to inform and help to set the public foreign policy agenda in areas in which an economic component is integral; and

- Training of the next generation of policymakers, who will require fluency in the workings of markets as well as the mechanics of international relations.

ABOUT THE AUTHORS

Alan P. Larson is a senior adviser at Covington & Burling, where he provides clients with strategic advice and counseling on international trade, finance, and antitrust/comity issues. Mr. Larson has been economic counselor to five secretaries of state since joining the U.S. Department of State in 1973. Most recently, Mr. Larson served as undersecretary of state for economic, business, and agricultural affairs and was the first foreign service officer to serve in this position. Prior to that, Mr. Larson served as ambassador to OECD in Paris. In addition to his role at Covington, Mr. Larson is a strategic adviser and director at the World Economic Forum and a distinguished fellow at the Council on Competitiveness. Mr. Larson is a member of the board of directors of the U.S. chapter of Transparency International. He has three degrees from the University of Iowa: a BA in political science, an MA in economics, and a PhD in economics.

David M. Marchick is a partner at Covington & Burling. He advises foreign investors and domestic companies seeking national security approval for foreign investments under the Exon-Florio amendment to the Defense Production Act of 1950. Mr. Marchick advised IBM in the sale of its personal computer division to Lenovo; Global Crossing with respect to the proposed investment from Hutchison Wampoa and completed investment from Singapore Technologies Telemedia; and BT in its acquisition of Infonet and has been active in the legislative debate over CFIUS reform as both an expert witness in testimony on behalf of U.S. and foreign companies. Mr. Marchick served as deputy assistant secretary of state for transportation affairs, where he was the senior U.S. negotiator for bilateral aviation agreements. Prior to this assignment, Mr. Marchick served as deputy assistant secretary for trade policy at the State Department and principal deputy assistant secretary of commerce for trade development. Mr. Marchick holds a BA in history from the University of California, San Diego, an MA in public policy from the Lyndon B. Johnson School of Public Affairs at the University of Texas at Austin, and a JD from George Washington University.

OTHER COUNCIL SPECIAL REPORTS
SPONSORED BY THE COUNCIL ON FOREIGN RELATIONS

Challenges for a Postelection Mexico: Issues for U.S. Policy
Pamela K. Starr; CSR No. 17, June 2006

U.S.-India Nuclear Cooperation: A Strategy for Moving Forward
Michael A. Levi and Charles N. Ferguson; CSR No. 16, June 2006

Generating Momentum for a New Era in U.S.-Turkey Relations
Steven A. Cook and Elizabeth Sherwood-Randall; CSR No. 15, June 2006

Peace in Papua: Widening a Window of Opportunity
Blair A. King; CSR No. 14, March 2006

Neglected Defense: Mobilizing the Private Sector to Support Homeland Security
Stephen E. Flynn and Daniel B. Prieto; CSR No. 13, March 2006

Afghanistan's Uncertain Transition From Turmoil to Normalcy
Barnett R. Rubin; CSR No. 12, March 2006

Preventing Catastrophic Nuclear Terrorism
Charles D. Ferguson; CSR No. 11, March 2006

Getting Serious About the Twin Deficits
Menzie D. Chinn; CSR No. 10, September 2005

Both Sides of the Aisle: A Call for Bipartisan Foreign Policy
Nancy E. Roman; CSR No. 9, September 2005

Forgotten Intervention? What the United States Needs to Do in the Western Balkans
Amelia Branczik and William L. Nash; CSR No. 8, June 2005

A New Beginning: Strategies for a More Fruitful Dialogue with the Muslim World
Craig Charney and Nicole Yakatan; CSR No. 7, May 2005

Power-Sharing in Iraq
David L. Phillips; CSR No. 6, April 2005

Giving Meaning to "Never Again": Seeking an Effective Response to the Crisis in Darfur and Beyond
Cheryl O. Igiri and Princeton N. Lyman; CSR No. 5, September 2004

Freedom, Prosperity, and Security: The G8 Partnership with Africa: Sea Island 2004 and Beyond
J. Brian Atwood, Robert S. Browne, and Princeton N. Lyman; CSR No. 4, May 2004

To purchase a hard copy, call the Brookings Institution Press: 800-537-5487.
Note: Council Special Reports are available on the Council's website at www.cfr.org. For more information, contact publications@cfr.org.

www.ingramcontent.com/pod-product-compliance
Lightning Source LLC
Chambersburg PA
CBHW051346290326
41933CB00042B/3310